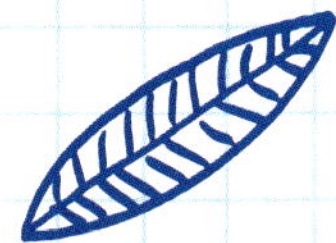

Table of Contents

Chapter One

Where Is Canada?

Imagine you are floating high above Earth. If you looked down on the planet, you would see some huge land areas surrounded by water. These land areas are called **continents**. Some continents are made up of several different countries. Canada is a huge country on the continent of North America.

This is a flat map of the Earth. Canada is inside the red circle.

You can drive across the border from the United States to Canada.

Canada

Elma Schemenauer

childsworld.com

Published by The Child's World®
800-599-READ · childsworld.com

Photography Credits
ID 85134145 © Lubomir Chudoba/Dreamstime.com, cover, 1; ID 142535595 © Iva Vanurova/Dreamstime.com, cover, 1 (inset); Tomas Kulaja/Shutterstock.com, 6; Gordon Pusnik/Shutterstock.com, 7; Lev Frid/Shutterstock.com, 8 (badger); Vlad G/Shutterstock.com, 8 (owl); Harry Collins Photography/Shutterstock.com, 8 (bighorn sheep); Pierre Leclerc/Shutterstock.com, 8 (black bear); Tony Campbell/Shutterstock.com, 9; ID 162444031 © Rpianoshow/Dreamstime.com, 10; Everett Collection/Newscom, 11; arindambanerjee/Shutterstock.com, 12; f11photo/Shutterstock.com, 13; Artem Zavarzin/Shutterstock.com, 14; VDV/Shutterstock.com, 15; R.M. Nunes/Shutterstock.com, 16; AdrianoK/Shutterstock.com, 17; Gorodenkoff/Shutterstock.com, 18; izikMD/Shutterstock.com, 19; Stephen Mcsweeny/Shutterstock.com, 20; Alessandro Cancian/Shutterstock.com, 21; Nalidsa/Shutterstock.com, 22; Michael L Brown/Shutterstock.com, 23; Maridav/Shutterstock.com, 24, 27; AdeJ Artventure/Shutterstock.com, 25; Eltonlaw/Shutterstock.com, 26; Beibeinside/Shutterstock.com, 28; Markus Wissmann/Shutterstock.com, 29; Lopolo/Shutterstock.com, 30

ISBN Information
9781503875982 (Reinforced Library Binding)
9781503876286 (Portable Document Format)
9781503876903 (Online Multi-user eBook)
9781503877405 (Electronic Publication)

LCCN
2025938578

Printed in the United States of America

About the Author

Elma Schemenauer was born near Elbow, Saskatchewan, where prairie life and her Mennonite roots sparked her imagination. After teaching for several years, Elma pursued a career in publishing and became the author of more than 75 books as well as numerous articles. When she's not writing, Elma enjoys reading, cooking, spending time with her family, and walking hillside trails near her home in Kamloops, British Columbia.

Cover: Moraine Lake is a famous glacial lake in Banff National Park in Alberta. Banff is Canada's first national park.

Canada stretches from the Pacific Ocean to the Atlantic Ocean. Canada is so big that it is divided into ten smaller parts called **provinces**. Provinces are a lot like American states. Canada also has three areas called **territories**. Canada's territories are huge areas in the north of Canada.

Did You Know?
Canada's territories are Yukon, Northwest Territories, and Nunavut.

Chapter Two

The Land

Since Canada is so big, there are many different kinds of land. Western Canada has many beautiful mountains. The Atlantic region is covered with grassy hills. Huge fields of crops stretch across Canada's Prairie Provinces—Alberta, Saskatchewan, and Manitoba. In the Eastern Lowlands, the weather is warm enough to grow apples and peaches.

Vancouver Island, off of Canada's Pacific Coast, is part of the province of British Columbia. It's known for its mild temperatures and beautiful scenery.

The Wabigoon River, in northwestern Ontario, flows through the cold, rocky Canadian Shield.

Another land area in Canada is called the Canadian Shield. Very few people live in this area because it is rocky and cold. In Canada's far north, it is windy and frozen most of the time. That's because the North Pole isn't very far away!

Did You Know?
Mount Logan in the Yukon Territory is the highest mountain in all of Canada. It stands 19,551 feet (5,959 meters) tall.

Chapter Three

Plants and Animals

Each area of Canada has its own kinds of plants and animals. Gophers and badgers live in the huge fields of the Prairie Provinces. In the Eastern Lowlands, hawks and owls soar high above the trees. The tall grasses of the Atlantic region are home to many rabbits and deer. Bighorn sheep live high in the mountain areas. And the beautiful Canadian Shield has thick forests that hide moose and bear.

Badger

Great gray owl

Bighorn sheep

Black bear

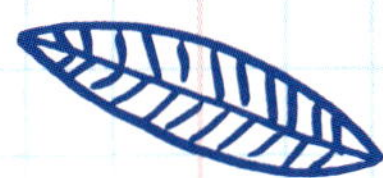

Most of the world's polar bears live in northern Canada.

The animals that live in Canada's far north have bodies that are specially made for living in cold temperatures. Polar bears have thick fur to keep them warm. And seals have a thick layer of fat that protects them from freezing weather.

Did You Know?

Canada is also home to several kinds of animals that are **endangered**. Some of them can only be found in Canada, such as the Newfoundland marten and the Vancouver Island marmot. Scientists and others are working to save these animals.

Chapter Four

Long Ago

The first people came to Canada thousands of years ago. Today, Canadians refer to these people as First Nations, **Inuit** (IN-yoo-it), and **Métis** (may-TEE). Many different First Nations have lived in parts of Canada for a long time. Some groups, such as the **Cree** (KREE), now live in Ontario, Quebec, and western Canada. The Inuit live across the Canadian north. In the past, these people hunted animals and farmed the land.

The Inuit have lived on Baffin Island for thousands of years. Baffin Island, in Nunavut, is the largest island in Canada.

French explorer Samuel de Champlain established the first French settlement in Canada in 1608.

Over the years, other people moved to Canada. People from France and Great Britain came in the 1500s and 1600s. They brought new languages and ways of life to Canada. But they also forced many **Indigenous** peoples off the land where they had lived for generations.

Chapter Five

Canada Today

Today, the people of Canada try to share the land, but sometimes there are problems. Sometimes First Nations peoples and other Canadians disagree about who owns the land or how the land should be used. Still they all work to live together peacefully despite their differences.

Did You Know?
Quebec is the largest province by area in Canada. It's the second-largest province by population.

First Nations peoples and others attend a protest in Toronto.

Tourists explore the quaint streets of Old Quebec, a historic neighborhood in Quebec City.

Sometimes English- and French-speaking Canadians have problems, too. The province of Quebec (kwuh-BEK) or (ki-BEK) is different from other Canadian provinces. Most people in Quebec speak French, and most people speak mainly English in the other areas. Some of the people in Quebec want their province to be a country of its own. Most of the other residents in Quebec, however, want Canada to stay together.

Chapter Six

The People

More than 38 million people live in Canada. Most of them live in the southern part of the country, where the temperatures are warmer. About one-third of all the people in Canada live in the province of Ontario. After Ontario, the largest Canadian provinces are Quebec and British Columbia.

Toronto, in southeastern Canada, is the capital of the province of Ontario.

Wearing traditional clothing, Canadians take part in a celebration honoring their history and culture.

Just like Americans, Canadians come from different backgrounds. Many Canadians have British or French backgrounds. Others have relatives that came from places such as Asia, Africa, Latin America, and the Caribbean. Canada's First Nations peoples are only a small part of the country's population. But they are growing fast. About 1.8 million Canadians have Indigenous **ancestry**.

Chapter Seven

City Life and Country Life

Life in Canada is very much like life in the United States. In the cities, people live in apartments or houses. They drive their cars or take the bus.

People can shop in supermarkets and shopping malls. In Canada's countryside, people live in houses just like ours. They drive their cars from place to place. Roads are good, and there are many small towns.

You can see beautiful fall scenery in Canada, like in this neighborhood in Montreal.

Traveling by dogsled is common in Yellowknife, which is located in the Northwest Territories.

In Canada's far north, life is very different. In the winter many roads are too rocky and rough for cars. Instead, some people use snowmobiles to go places. Where there aren't roads, people use airplanes and boats to move around. Some people even travel by dogsled in the far north. Mostly, though, dogsleds are used for fun or for racing.

Did You Know?
Canada goes so far north that it almost reaches the North Pole!

Chapter Eight

Schools and Language

Canadian schools are much like American schools. Children start kindergarten when they are about five years old. They learn reading, writing, and math. Students also study science, social studies, and music, just as you do. And many Canadian children do their schoolwork on laptops, just like children in the United States.

English and French are official languages at many public schools throughout the country.

Ottawa, the national capital of Canada, has road signs in both English and French.

English and French are both official languages in Canada. All Canadians learn at least a little bit of each language in school. In Quebec, students spend more time on French since that's the province's main language. In New Brunswick, both languages are important since a lot of people there speak English and French. In parts of Canada, road signs must be written in both languages for everyone to understand them.

Chapter Nine

Work

There are many kinds of jobs in Canada. In the cities, many people work in offices, factories, hospitals, and stores. In the countryside, farmers grow crops and raise animals.

Dairy and beef cattle are major industries in Canada.

Lobster traps are stacked on a dock in Nova Scotia, which is on Canada's east coast along the Atlantic Ocean.

Loggers cut trees from the forests to make paper and buildings. Along the seashore, people sell fish, lobsters, and clams. In the far north, people hunt, fish, and trap animals for their furs.

Did You Know?
Canadians call their dollar coins "loonies." That's because the coin has a bird called a loon on the back.

Chapter Ten

Food

Canadians eat lots of different foods. Supermarkets in Canada have everything from microwave popcorn to canned soups. Many Canadians still eat dishes their long-ago relatives, or ancestors, enjoyed. They eat corn and beans like some of the First Nations peoples. They make pea soup like the early French settlers. And they eat beef and drink tea like the early British settlers. Canadians also eat plenty of foods brought by newer settlers. Restaurants in Canada serve everything from Italian pasta to Chinese egg rolls.

People enjoy grilled salmon during a national day celebration in Richmond, British Columbia.

Poutine originated in Quebec in the late 1950s.

Did You Know?
The unofficial national dish of Canada is poutine (poo-TEEN). Poutine is french fries mixed with cheese curds and covered in a brown gravy.

Chapter Eleven

Pastimes

Because much of the country has long, cold winters, Canadians play many winter sports. Children slide down snow-covered hills on long sleds called **toboggans**. Children in Canada also like to snowshoe, ski, skate, and play ice hockey—just like American kids! In summer, children like bike riding, roller-skating, and swimming. Soccer, baseball, football, lacrosse, and basketball are popular team sports. Many families like to camp in Canada's beautiful mountains and countryside. And for those who like the city, there are plenty of shows to see and museums to visit.

Mont Tremblant is a well-known ski resort in the mountains of Quebec.

Hiking is a popular pastime in Canada. There are trails with breathtaking views throughout the country.

Did You Know?
Canada has more than 40 national parks where people can go hiking, camping, fishing, and more.

Chapter Twelve

Holidays

Canadians and Americans have many of the same holidays. Both countries celebrate Christmas, New Year's, and Halloween. Canadians celebrate their country's birthday, too. On Canada Day, July 1, people fly Canada's red-and-white maple-leaf flag. They hold parades and picnics, and shoot off fireworks. Canada Day is a lot like the Fourth of July in the United States.

Children in Toronto celebrate Canada Day at a parade.

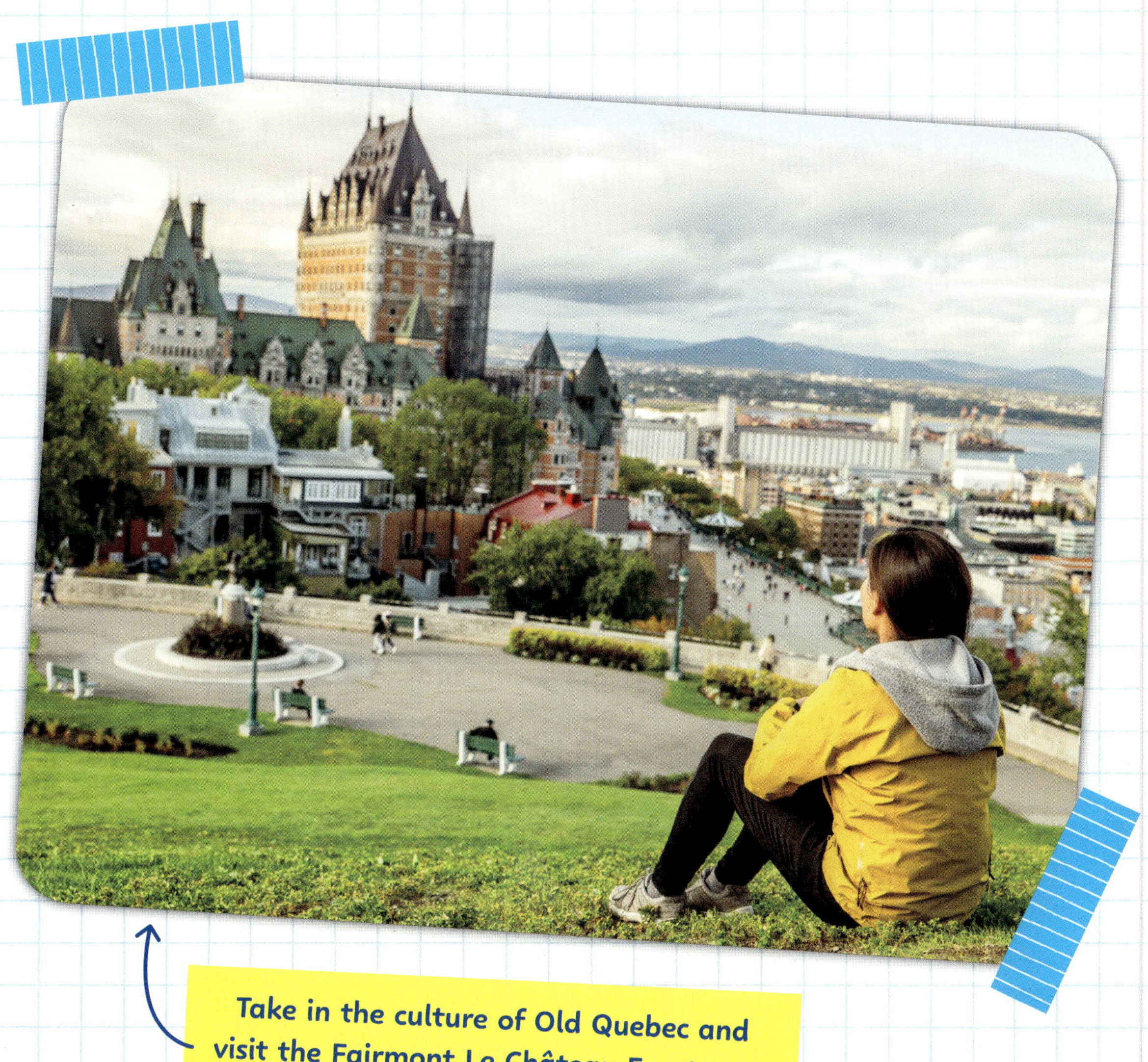

Take in the culture of Old Quebec and visit the Fairmont Le Château Frontenac, a historic hotel on the St. Lawrence River.

Canada is a huge country with many special things to see and do. Maybe one day you will visit Toronto to catch a Toronto Maple Leafs ice hockey game. Or perhaps you'll go snowboarding in Whistler, a famous ski resort north of Vancouver. Or maybe you'll watch a huge polar bear roam across the Arctic ice. Wherever you go, Canada is sure to be an interesting place!

Fast Facts About Canada

Area: 3,849,674 square miles (9,970,610 square kilometers); this is a little larger than the United States

Population: About 38,794,813 people

Capital City: Ottawa

Head of Government: The prime minister of Canada

Head of State: The king or queen of the United Kingdom and their representative, the governor general

Other Important Cities: Toronto, Montreal, Vancouver, Edmonton

Money: Canadian dollar; the Canadian dollar is divided into 100 cents

National Flag: A red and white flag with a red maple leaf in the center; the maple leaf is Canada's national symbol

National Animal: The beaver

National Holiday: Canada Day on July 1; Canada Day is a lot like the Fourth of July in the United States

National Colors: Red and white

National Song: "O Canada" is the national anthem of Canada. It is sung in English and French.

O Canada! Our home and native land!
True patriot love in all thy sons command.
With glowing hearts we see thee rise,
The True North strong and free!
From far and wide,
O Canada, we stand on guard for thee.
God keep our land glorious and free!
O Canada, we stand on guard for thee.
O Canada, we stand on guard for thee.

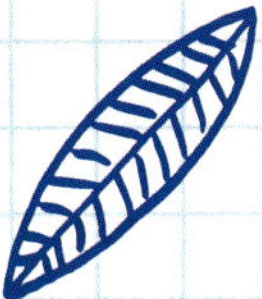

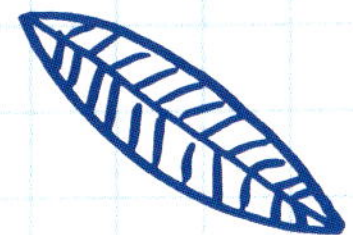

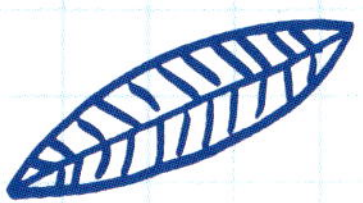

Famous People:

Margaret Atwood: author

Frederick Banting: Nobel Prize–winning scientist

Justin Bieber: pop and R&B singer-songwriter, producer

Roberta Bondar: astronaut, neurologist, first Canadian woman in space

Tommy Douglas: politician, founder of the country's universal health care system

Wayne Gretzky: ice hockey player

Mike Myers: comedian, actor

Michael Ondaatje: author

Lester B. Pearson: politician, diplomat, Nobel Peace Prize winner

David Suzuki: scientist, author, television host

Justin Trudeau: former prime minister, politician (and son of Pierre Trudeau, who also served as prime minister)

Hayley Wickenheiser: ice hockey player, Olympic gold medalist

Canadian Folklore:

O Kanata!
In 1535, an explorer got lost and two Indigenous children told the explorer about a village that was close by. The word in their language was *kanata*. When the explorer got back to his friends, he told them about the land he had visited—only he called it "Canada," instead. That is how Canada got its name!

Margaret Atwood

How Do You Say . . .

English	French	How to Say It
hello	bonjour	bohn-ZSHOOR
goodbye	au revoir	OH ruh-VWAR
please	s'il vous plaît	seel voo PLAY
thank you	merci	mayr-SEE
one	un	UNH
two	deux	DOO
three	trois	TWAH
Canada	Canada	KAH-nah-dah
Quebec	Quebec	keh-BEK

Glossary

ancestry (ANN-ses-tree) Ancestry means that a person has ancestors, or relatives from long ago. The ancestors of many Canadians came from places like Asia and Europe.

continents (KON-tih-nents) Most of the land areas on Earth are in huge sections called continents. Canada is a country on the continent of North America.

Cree (KREE) One of Canada's Indigenous peoples who live in Ontario, Quebec, and western Canada.

endangered (en-DAYN-jurd) When a species or plant is in danger of no longer existing, it is endangered.

Indigenous (in-DIJ-uh-nuss) Indigenous peoples are the earliest known people who lived in a place.

Inuit (IN-yoo-it) One of Canada's Indigenous peoples who live in the northern part of Canada.

Métis (may-TEE) One of Canada's Indigenous peoples who live in western Canada.

provinces (PRO-vin-sez) Provinces are districts or regions of a country. Canada is divided into ten smaller sections called provinces.

territories (TAYR-uh-tor-eez) Territories are large areas of land under the control of a nation or state. Canada's three territories are huge areas in the north of Canada.

toboggans (tuh-BAH-gunz) Toboggans are long sleds that are curved up at one end. Many toboggans are made of thin pieces of wood, but some are made from metal or plastic.

For More Information

READ IT

Kesselring, Susan, and Elisa Chavarri (illustrator). *National Day Traditions Around the World*. Parker, CO: The Child's World, 2022.

Lin, Chelsea. *Weird but True! Canada: 300 Outrageous Facts About the True North*. Washington, DC: National Geographic Kids, 2018.

Miller, Susan Hoskins. *Canada*. Parker, CO: The Child's World, 2016.

Saint-Claire, Esta. *Canada*. New York, NY: PowerKids Press, 2024.

LOOK IT UP

Visit our website for lots of links about Canada:

childsworld.com/links

Note to Parents, Caregivers, Teachers, and Librarians: We routinely verify our web links to make sure they are safe, active sites—so encourage your readers to check them out!

Index